NATURAL WORLD

HIPPOPOTAMUS

HABITATS • LIFE CYCLES • FOOD CHAINS • THREATS

Michael Leach

an imprint of Hodder Children's Books

Produced in Association with WWF-UK

NATURAL WORLD

Chimpanzee • Crocodile • Dolphin • Elephant • Giant Panda
Great White Shark • Grizzly Bear • Hippopotamus
Killer Whale • Lion • Orangutan • Penguin • Polar Bear • Tiger

Produced for Hodder Wayland by
Roger Coote Publishing
Gissing's Farm, Fressingfield
Suffolk IP21 5SH, UK

WWF is a registered charity no. 201707
WWF-UK, Panda House, Weyside Park
Godalming, Surrey GU7 1XR

Cover: A hippo 'yawning'.
Title page: An adult hippo in feeding grounds.
Contents page: Another hippo 'yawns'.
Index page: Surfacing through a layer of water lettuce.

Series editor: Polly Goodman
Designer: Michael Posen
Cover designer: Victoria Webb

Published in paperback in 2001 by Hodder Wayland,
an imprint of Hodder Children's Books

A Catalogue record for this book is available from the British Library.

ISBN 0 7502 30517

Printed and bound by G. Canale & C. S.p.A. Turin, Italy

Hodder Children's Books
A division of Hodder Headline Limited
338 Euston Road, London NW1 3BH

Picture acknowledgements
Biofotos 7, (Geoff Moon), 8 (Heather Angel), 16–17 (Heather Angel), 23 (Heather Angel), 28 (Heather Angel), 29 (Heather Angel), 30 (Heather Angel), 31 (Heather Angel), 44 bottom (Heather Angel); Bruce Coleman Collection *Cover* (Jorg Petra Wegner), 11 (Leonard Lee Rue), 14, 17 (Uwe Walz), 18 (MR Phicton), 19 Jen & Des Bartlett), 35 (Mark N Boulton), 42 (Andrew Purcell), 43 Mark N Boulton), 45 top (Uwe Walz); Digital Vision 1, 27, 41, 45 bottom; Michael Leach 38; Oxford Scientific Films 6 (Rafi Ben-Shahar), 12 (Tom Leach), 14–15 (Norbert Rosing), 22 (Joan Root), 24 (Daniel J Cox), 26 (Alan Root), 33 (Hilary Pooley), 34 (Richard Packwood), 39 (Peter Cook), 40 (Hilary Pooley), 44 middle (Tom Leach), 48 (Norbert Rosing); Stock Market 37 (Tom Brakefield), 45 middle (Tom Brakefield); Still Pictures 10 (S Krasemann), 44 top (S Krasemann); Tony Stone Images 3 (Peter/Stef Lamberti), 9 (Art Wolfe), 13 (Manoj Shah), 20 (John Warden), 21 (John Warden), 32 (Daryl Balfour), 36 (Gary Vesta). Map on page 4 by Victoria Webb. All other artwork by Michael Posen.

Contents

Meet the Hippo

Hippos are plump, barrel-shaped animals that live in rivers and lakes. They live together in herds among the grasslands of Africa, south of the Sahara Desert.

A hippo's eyes, ears and nostrils are at the top of its skull, so it can breathe and be aware of everything around it while most of its body stays underwater. A sleeping hippo in the water can be difficult to see, with only the top of its head visible. If disturbed, the only movement may be its ears swivelling round to face the source of the sound. When frightened, it will silently sink underwater and completely disappear.

▼ **The red shading on this map shows where hippos live in Africa.**

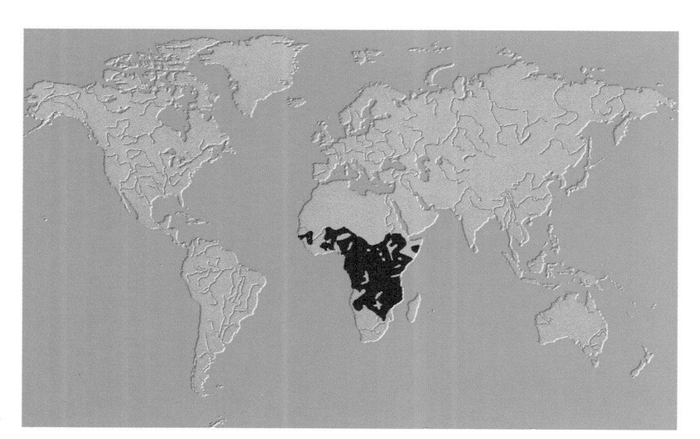

Skin and fat

Hippos have very sensitive skin, which can easily be burnt by the sun. They wallow in water and mud for protection. Skin makes up nearly 25 per cent of the entire weight of a hippo. The layer of fat on the sides and back of a hippo can be 5 centimetres thick.

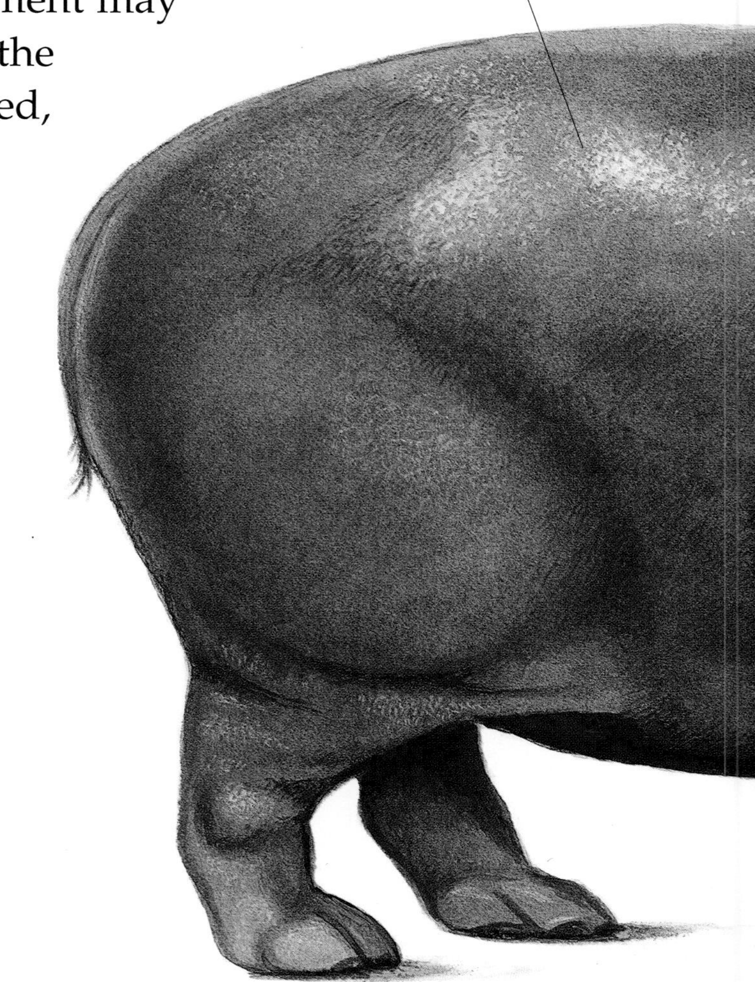

HIPPOPOTAMUS FACTS

Hippos grow up to 3.4 metres long and 1.4 metres high. Males are known as bulls and weigh up to 3,200 kilograms. Females are known as cows and weigh up to 1,400 kilograms.

●

The Latin name for the hippo is *Hippopotamus amphibius*. 'Hippopotamus' means water-horse, but the hippo is not a horse. It is a distant relative of the pig family.

Nostrils
Hippos have a good sense of smell. They can close their nostrils underwater.

Ears
Hippos have small ears, which they can close to stop water entering when they go underwater.

Eyes
Hippos have small eyes and poor eyesight. Their eyes are designed to see both above and below water.

Hair
A hippo's body is bald apart from a few stiff bristles around the mouth and some hairs at the end of the tail.

Teeth
The hippo's lower canine teeth are extremely sharp and can measure up to 50 centimetres long. Canine teeth are not used for feeding. They are weapons of defence or attack.

Feet
Hippos have four webbed feet, which act as paddles to help them swim.

Jaws
A hippo's huge jaws are powered by strong muscles. A single bite from a hippo can crush a fully grown crocodile.

Relatives

Fossil evidence shows that there were once several species of hippo. The family evolved about 10 million years ago and spread throughout much of Europe and Asia.

Today, only the common hippo and the pygmy hippo are alive. The common hippo is found over large areas of central and southern Africa. Its smaller cousin, the pygmy hippo, lives only in West Africa.

◀ **The pygmy hippo is often hunted by large predators such as leopards. Just like its larger cousin, the pygmy hippo uses long canine teeth to defend itself against attack.**

▲ **This pygmy hippo is underwater, patrolling its territory to keep away rivals of the same species. Each hippo carries out this duty every day.**

The pygmy hippo is about the size of a sheep. It lives in lakes and rivers surrounded by thick forest. Unlike their larger cousins, pygmy hippos do not live in herds. They are solitary animals that come together only to mate.

For centuries the pygmy hippo has been hunted for meat and has now become an endangered species. They are very wary of humans, which makes them difficult to study. There is still a lot that scientists do not understand about the behaviour of the pygmy hippo.

Habitat

Apart from coming out every night to feed, hippos' lives are based entirely around water. They cannot survive without the cool shelter of deep rivers and lakes. Hippos prefer still or slow-moving water because fast-flowing rivers could carry them away while they are asleep.

▲ Hippos sometimes rest on small river islands to avoid humans, but they rarely stay long because there is not enough food available on these tiny patches of land.

Hippos are nocturnal animals and they have a simple routine. Their days are spent in the water and their nights are spent on land. They have evolved to exist well in both environments. A hippo's short, powerful legs can run surprisingly quickly on land, while underwater they can be used for swimming. Every 24 hours, hippos spend six hours eating and the other 18 hours dozing in the water.

▶ On hot sunny days, a hippo will stay like this for many hours. Just the top of its head can be seen and it will come up to breathe about once every five minutes.

A Hippo is Born

Eight months after mating, a female hippo moves away from the rest of the herd, looking for a private place to give birth. She looks for a sheltered stretch of water, or a rough bed of grass and reeds built on the riverbank near the water's edge.

Most hippo births take place in very shallow water, which only reaches the mother's stomach. In deeper water, the calf must immediately rise to the surface to breathe. Many calves that are born underwater drown in their first few minutes of life.

◀ The skin of the young calf is much pinker than that of its mother. New-born hippos are equally at home on land or in water.

◀ A hippo calf stays very close to its mother for the first few weeks of its life. They spend most of their time touching each other to cut down the chance of being separated.

The new-born hippo calf can stand up within an hour and starts suckling almost at once. It can walk on wobbly feet and swim soon afterwards. The mother hippo and her calf live apart from the herd for up to fourteen days after the birth to protect the new-born calf from being accidentally crushed by the huge adults.

HIPPO CALVES

New-born hippo calves weigh about 45 kilograms and are pink at birth. They change colour immediately after birth and are grey by the time they are a month old.

•

Normally just one calf is born, but occasionally there are twins. When two calves are born, one is likely to die within a few days.

First food

At about four weeks, the calf will try its first solid food. It begins by nibbling soft grass and slowly learns to find other vegetation. The calf continues to suckle its mother's milk until it is about ten months old.

Suckling normally happens on dry land, but the calf sometimes feeds underwater by holding its breath and sucking. Most calves are born in the rainy season, when there is plenty of fresh grass to be found. So the female eats well and produces a good supply of milk for her quickly growing calf.

▲ Hippo calves are tiny compared to their huge mothers. To reach full adult body weight a young hippo needs to eat a vast amount of food in its early years.

Very young calves lie on their mother's back in the river. When they get too hot, they slide into the water for a while and then clamber back on.

▲ In a large herd there may be many newly born hippos. Females identify their own calf by its individual scent.

Keeping safe

Female hippos are extremely protective mothers and will attack any animal that comes too close to their calf. The mother needs to be very alert because hippos often share the river with crocodiles. These giant reptiles would never challenge an adult hippo, but they are always on the look-out for an unprotected calf.

If the calf leaves its mother's side, a crocodile can quickly strike from underwater, grabbing the young calf and pulling it under to drown.

◀ **A mother and her calf on the edge of a crocodile-infested pool. You can just see the scales of a crocodile on the surface of the water.**

The calf is not safe on dry land either. Every night, the young hippo follows its mother as she leaves the river to feed on grasslands nearby. These lands are home to predators such as hyenas and leopards. They have learned to wait until the female hippo lowers her head to eat before darting in and grabbing the calf. But they must be quick. If the mother catches their scent, she will immediately charge and give a deadly bite.

CALF DEATHS

About 45 per cent of young hippos die before they reach the age of one year.

▼ **Crocodiles may look slow and clumsy but they can move incredibly quickly. On land they can easily outrun a human, and a hippo calf away from its mother is an easy meal to catch.**

Learning to Survive

When the young hippo calf first joins the herd, it has to avoid being accidentally trampled underfoot, or crushed between two adults. As it grows, the calf becomes more nimble and can quickly move away if an adult becomes aggressive.

▼ Hippos normally only leave the water when the sun is low and the temperature is dropping.

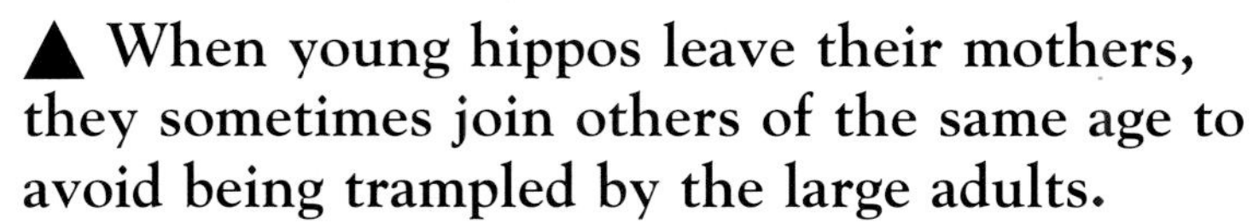

▲ **When young hippos leave their mothers, they sometimes join others of the same age to avoid being trampled by the large adults.**

At the first sign of danger, the calf immediately returns to its mother's side. But if she is out of reach it will quickly dive and stand still on the riverbed.

At first the calf can only hide in the water for 30 or 40 seconds before it runs out of breath. But slowly it learns how to stay underwater for several minutes.

▼ The pink mucus that hippo skin produces probably has an antibiotic effect, which helps keep it clean in the dirty water of a hippo river.

Avoiding the sun

The young hippo must quickly learn to master life in the water if it is to survive. Rivers and lakes provide essential shelter for the young hippo because its skin is extremely sensitive to sunburn. Water passes through a hippo's skin five times faster than humans, and faster than any other animal. So without shelter, the hippo would soon dehydrate and eventually die.

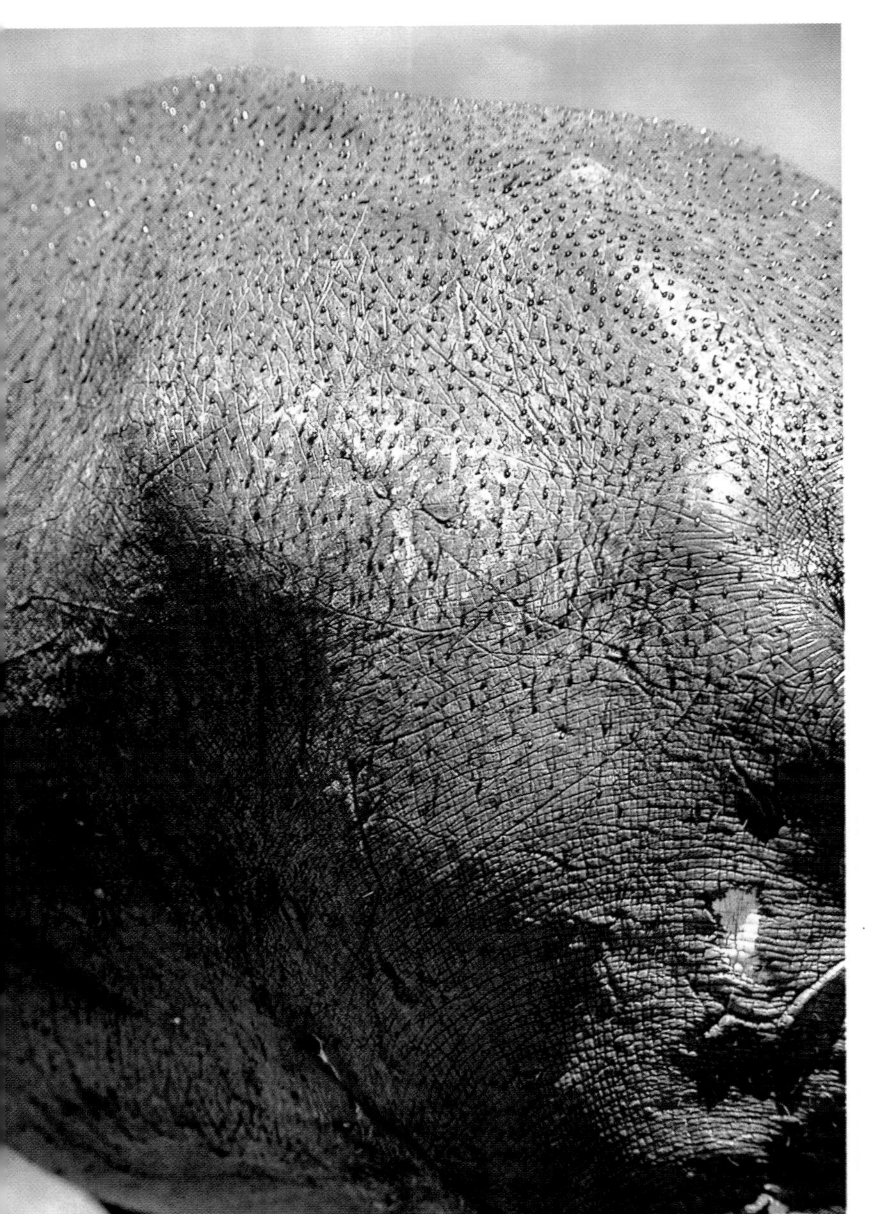

THE LEGEND OF HIPPO BLOOD

Hippo skin produces a pink mucus, which acts as a type of sunblock. The mucus absorbs ultra-violet rays that cause sunburn and moisturise the hippo's skin, preventing it from drying and cracking when out of the water. Early travellers who saw this pink mucus thought it was blood, and told tales of strange river animals that sweated blood.

In tropical Africa, daytime temperatures can reach 38° C, so the hippos keep cool by spending their days sleeping in the water. During the day they lie submerged with only the tops of their heads showing. They can remain completely still for hours on end, their only movement an occasional yawn.

During the day, the dominant males in the herd take the most sheltered spots, often close to a riverbank beneath overhanging branches. The others are forced to find less comfortable places.

▼ Some dry seasons last a long time. When rains are late, rivers become very low or sometimes even disappear. If the water vanishes, hippos wallow in mud to keep cool. The mud dries into a thick hard layer, which keeps off the worst of the sun's rays.

◀ Hippos will investigate anything new underwater. Since they have poor eyesight, they need to get close for a good view. This hippo is examining the photographer at close range.

Diving

Occasionally, the hippo will disappear underwater and come back up a long way from where it vanished. Usually, the hippo walks slowly on the riverbed, but if it is frightened or angry, it will swim. Hippos prefer rivers that have gently sloping banks and are deep in the middle, which allows them to completely disappear underwater if they are threatened.

▲ A lot of hippo behaviour is hidden from view underwater. These two adults are testing each other's strength, which prepares them for more serious battles in the future.

Although hippos are huge, they can move surprisingly quickly in water. Their huge weight is partly supported by the water, which makes movement much easier than on land. When the hippo comes back up to the surface, it breathes out violently with a loud explosion of sound that can be heard all around the river.

ESCAPE

Hippos dive underwater when threatened. Most dives last between 3 to 5 minutes, but hippos have been known to stay underwater for up to 12 minutes.

Finding Food

When it is about ten months old, the young hippo becomes completely weaned and must rely entirely on vegetation for food. Every night the hippo, along with the rest of the herd, stays in the water until after sunset. When the sun has disappeared, it clambers up the riverbank and follows the herd on their trail to find food, travelling up to 3.2 kilometres from the river to a good feeding ground.

The hippo's main food is grass, which it plucks with wide delicate lips. Standing in one spot, the hippo slowly moves its head from side to side, grazing all the food within reach, before walking on a few steps and starting again. Hippos are noisy eaters. Their chomping and grunting can be heard up to 46 metres away.

▼ Hippos and catfish share the last drops of mud in a dried-out lake in Tanzania. When the mud finally dries out, the hippos will leave to look for new water and the catfish will die.

HIPPO LAWNS

Hippo feeding grounds are easy to find. They crop the grass low to the ground, leaving just a short turf. This creates huge open areas called 'hippo lawns'. Hippo lawns are perfect for other grazers such as antelope, which have much smaller mouths to eat the grass that the hippos miss. Small grazers are often seen feeding on hippo lawns during the day.

▲ Grassland next to water is ideal feeding ground for hippos.

For the first ten months of its life, the young hippo stays close to its mother while she is feeding. After ten months, when it is weaned, the hippo will become much more independent and will spread out among the other members of the herd.

The hippo diet

Although grass makes up the bulk of their diet, hippos eat a wide variety of other vegetation including leaves, fallen fruit and tree bark. A large herd of hippos has a huge effect on the vegetation around the river simply because they eat so much. When a hippo herd grows too big, they can overgraze an area and kill the grass, leaving nothing to eat.

HIPPO APPETITES

Hippos are completely herbivorous. Each animal can eat up to 50 kilograms of food a night.

▼ Hippos only feed on ground-level plants or bushes up to shoulder height. The trees around hippo lawns often have no leaves below 1.5 metres high. Above this height, the leaves grow thick because the hippos cannot reach them.

HIPPOPOTAMUS
FOOD CHAIN

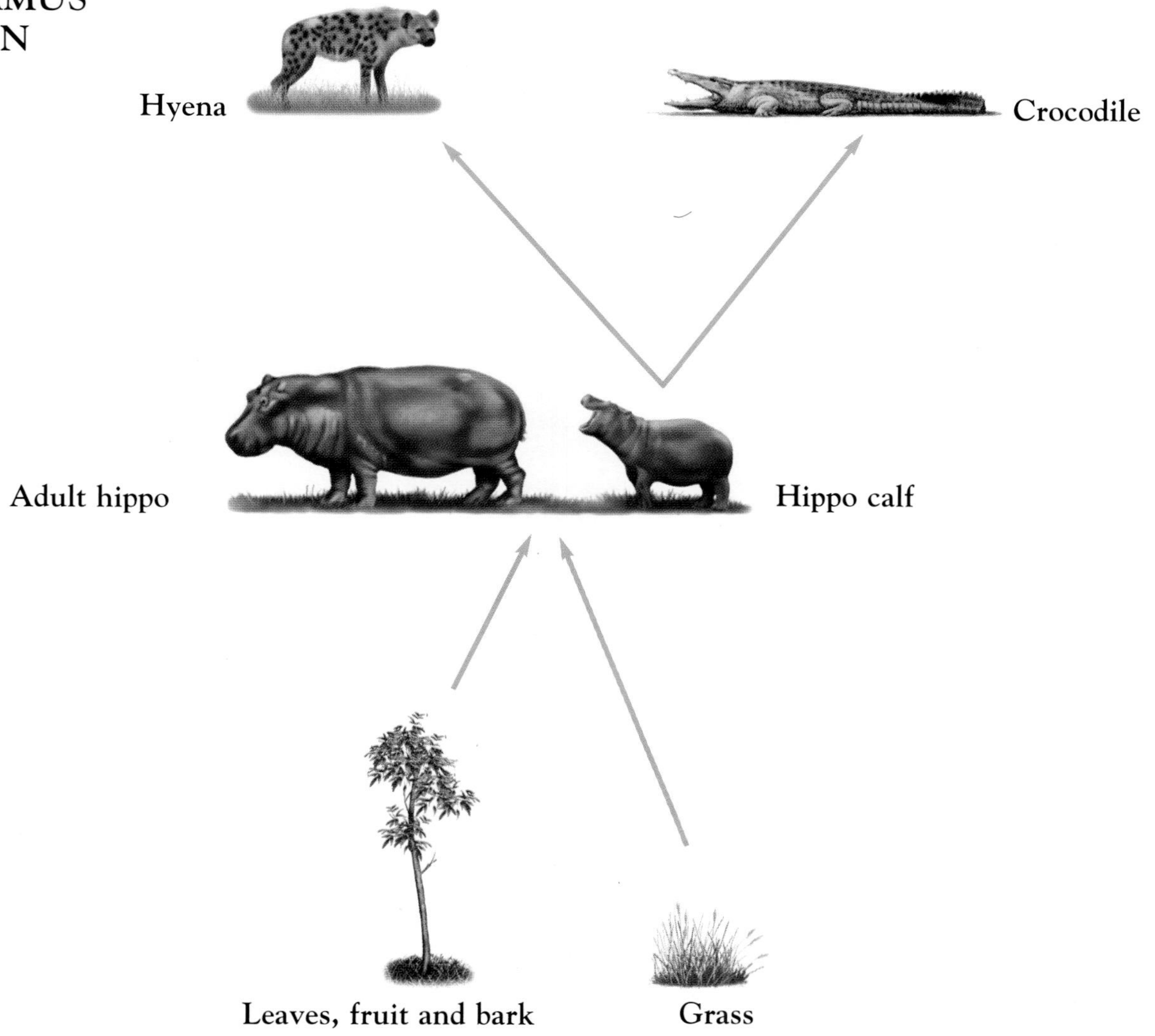

▲ **Healthy, adult hippos are too fierce to be preyed upon. Calves that stray from their mother's side may be attacked by crocodiles, leopards or hyenas.**

When food is scarce, hippos usually move along the river to find new feeding grounds. Sometimes they leave the river for a short time to look for new feeding grounds, but there has to be another stretch of water or mudhole nearby where they can spend the day in safety. Hippos cannot travel far from the river without running the risk of being stranded out of water when the sun rises.

Hippos and the environment

Hippos help support a variety of other living creatures in their habitat. A herd of hippos produces an enormous amount of dung, which is normally dropped directly into the river. Hippo dung is a perfect fertiliser that enriches the water and speeds up the growth of aquatic plants. The fertile water also encourages algae to live on the hippo's skin.

▶ This cattle egret is catching some of the flies that always gather around large animals in Africa. The hippo accepts the bird because the flies are a nuisance.

The plants and algae provide extra food for a variety of animals. Small fish eat the water plants and nibble the algae on the hippos' skin. The fish provide food for birds such as egrets, kingfishers and herons.

The hippo herd also attracts swarms of flies, which are eagerly snapped up by small birds. So the entire river benefits enormously from hippos and without them, an African river would be a very different habitat.

▼ Fish eating algae from a hippo's skin.

Hippo trails

Hippos are creatures of habit and use the same trails every night to reach their feeding grounds. The trails are impossible to miss because the hippos' huge feet and weight squash the soil so that nothing can grow.

Hippos mark the trail with piles of dung, which they use as scent signposts to find their way back to the river. They like to have a clear route to safety and become very aggressive if the trail is blocked. A hippo will attack any animal that stands on their path back to the river. By following the rest of the herd every night, the young hippo learns to find the best feeding grounds.

◀ Hippo footprints showing the route from the river to the hippo lawn. The prints clearly show each of the hippo's four toes.

During the rainy season, there is lots of food. But when the rains finish, the grass stops growing and is almost completely burned away by the sun. By the end of the dry season there may be nothing left for the hippos to eat. Sometimes they will dig with their mouths to reach roots and bulbs underground. This provides a little food but in times of drought, hippos can go several weeks without eating. Only their reserves of body fat keep them alive.

▼This hippo is carrying a clump of water lettuce on its back. This accidental behaviour helps spread water plants between rivers and lakes.

Life in the Herd

As the hippo grows up, it must find its natural place in the herd. Each herd is made up of a single dominant male, females with young and non-breeding males. The herd lives together very peacefully until the breeding season begins. Then the males start to fight and compete for the right to mate.

HIPPO HERDS

Herds usually contain between ten and fifteen hippos, but herds of 150 hippos have been found. Fighting is much more common in large herds because there is more competition.

•

Each dominant male controls a length of up to 300 metres of riverbank.

▼ A herd of hippos in a river in Zambia.

The dominant male constantly patrols his territory. If a rival male approaches, he will challenge him, staring at him without moving. Then, sweeping his tail from side to side, the hippo drops dung and sprays it behind him. This spreads his scent around to warn away the rival.

▲Spraying dung spreads the scent of a hippo over a large area. This is a sign that warns off any rivals that may want to move into the territory.

If the challenging male still does not leave, the dominant hippo yawns widely to show his teeth. Hippos can open their mouths to an incredible angle of 150 degrees. If the rival male is confident, he will reply by copying the yawn to show off his own teeth.

Fighting

Rival males begin fighting by charging at each other and touching mouths, both still with their jaws wide open. They each push hard to test the other's strength and one might suddenly back off if he realises his rival is stronger.

If neither surrenders, the display becomes more aggressive. The hippos sink into the water and reappear suddenly, rearing up on their back legs and splashing down in front of their rival. The hippos use their huge mouths to scoop up water and throw it violently.

▼ **Fighting males can sometimes disappear from view in a shower of splashing water.**

AGGRESSIVE MALES

In the breeding season, male hippos are so aggressive and protective of their territory they will attack any animal or human that comes too close. Even young calves can be killed.

▶ Hippo battles are always violent and sometimes fatal. If this male uses his canine teeth to puncture his rival's throat, death would quickly follow.

Most fights are solved at this stage, but if the two hippos are evenly matched, the fight becomes violent. Hippo fights are vicious, and usually end with both animals injured. Sometimes the battle only ends when one is killed. Hippos fight with their teeth. Sometimes they bite, but they also slash sideways to cut open the opponent's skin.

Battle scars

Most fights end when the weaker male realizes he cannot beat his rival. The stronger hippo is left to take ownership of the territory. Defeated males sometimes leave the herd and join other males in bachelor groups. Often these animals never get the chance to breed because only males with territories will mate.

▼ The canine teeth in the top jaw are slightly further back than those in the lower jaw. This allows the teeth to work like huge scissors that cut through flesh and produce terrible injuries.

Male hippos have extra-thick skin on their sides, which protects them from the very worst injuries. But even with this padding they still suffer terrible wounds. All adult male hippos clearly show the scars left from dominance battles and the skin of older animals is covered with a tangle of white lines and holes where razor-sharp teeth once bit.

▲ Adult male hippos are usually badly scarred, but most of the damage is just to their skin. Their insides are protected from real injury.

Female hippos are not involved in territorial battles. They keep well away from the fighting males and behave as if nothing is happening.

HIPPO NOISES

When excited or frightened, a hippo produces a high-pitched neigh, which sounds like a horse. Males fighting for dominance have a powerful bull-like bellow. The mating call is three short coughs. An angry hippo grinds its teeth loudly.

Finding a mate

Male hippos can mate when they reach the age of five, but they may be ten years old before they are strong enough to win their own territory. The dominant male of a herd will mate with any female who enters his territory. Other males will be immediately attacked if they attempt to mate.

MATING

A female hippo usually has one calf every 18–24 months. She may mate again within two months of giving birth. She will give birth to about ten calves during her life. After mating, male hippos play no part in rearing the calves.

●

Only dominant males holding territory will mate. A healthy male hippo will stay in one territory for up to eight years.

▼ Pushing muzzles helps rival males judge the strength of a rival. The weaker animal often backs off before fighting begins.

Mating takes place in the water and the process is over in minutes. Most mating happens in the dry season when rivers are small and the hippos are close together in the water.

▲ Fighting males always try to bite the neck of a rival, which is the most vulnerable part of a hippo.

Female hippos start breeding at about seven years old. Throughout her adult life, a female hippo is either pregnant or caring for a calf, often both at the same time.

Threats

The adult hippo's huge size and powerful bite will drive away most predators, so most hippos die of old age instead of being killed.

Hippos in a herd are especially safe. But if one hippo becomes separated from the rest of the herd, it might be stalked by a pride of lions. The hippo will defend itself by putting up a fight, often badly injuring the lions before they manage to kill their prey.

▼ Crocodiles are the largest predators in Africa's waterways. Together with humans they are the hippos' most dangerous enemy.

▲ This hippo has been killed for food in Malawi. Its body will be cut up and the meat taken back to the village. The remains will be eaten by vultures and hyenas.

UNDER THREAT

Hippos are officially listed as a species 'under threat', which means that the population is much lower than it once was. But they are not yet an 'endangered species', which would mean that they are in danger of extinction.

The hippo's main threat, however, is from humans. People kill hippos for many different reasons. Hippo meat is highly prized in some areas. It can be cooked fresh or cut into strips and dried in the sunshine. Hippo skin is flexible and hard-wearing. Farmers use it to make cattle whips, known in Africa as 'sjamboks'. These are valuable and poachers have been known to kill hippos just to make whips from their skin.

Hippos are also killed for the ivory that forms their canine teeth. Unlike elephants' tusks, hippo ivory does not turn yellow with age, so it is highly prized and extremely valuable.

◀ This 'yawn' is actually a display to show the power and weapons of a hippo.

Dangerous hippos

Hippos living close to villages are sometimes killed to protect people, because they can be very dangerous. After the mosquito, hippos kill more humans than any other animal in Africa. Most people think that Africa's most dangerous animals are predators such as lions and crocodiles. But these large carnivores are actually frightened of humans and will avoid contact. Hippos, however, are very aggressive and will charge even when they are not being threatened.

▲ Hippos are at their most dangerous when they are underwater and can't be seen. This one is just being curious and is unlikely to attack.

Hippo attacks usually happen without warning and most take place in the water. Swimmers, fishermen and even people washing clothes in a river can be attacked for no obvious reason. Hippos have also been known to turn over small boats by hitting them from under the water. Once in the river, a person is easily killed with a single bite from the hippo's huge mouth.

▲ When rivers are low, hippos are forced to gather together in the last pools of deep water.

Too many hippos

Sometimes hippos raid farmland to eat crops such as corn and sugar cane. A herd can wipe out an entire harvest in a single night. Once hippos have discovered this food they keep returning, so farmers kill them to protect their crops.

In national parks where hippo hunting is banned, numbers of hippos can sometimes grow too large. A herd of 150 animals can eat nearly 7.4 tonnes of food in just six hours. This threatens the food supply of other grazing animals and some countries now shoot the older hippos to keep the population down.

TOURISTS AND ZOOS

Hippos are popular tourist attractions in national parks in Uganda and Kenya, particularly in the Masai Mara National Park, where there is a healthy population of hippos. Up to a hundred tour buses a day can visit an accessible herd.

•

Hippos are also kept in many zoos around the world. They often breed successfully in captivity and can live for up to 45 years. Zoos around the world regularly exchange hippos to provide new mates. This guarantees that the animals do not breed with close relatives and keeps the population healthy.

▼ Hippos are one of the most popular tourist attractions in national parks such as the Masai Mara in Kenya.

Hippo Life Cycle

New-born hippos have pink skin and weigh about 45 kilograms.

For the first few weeks the mother and baby hippo stay away from the main herd.

The young hippo joins the herd and takes its first solid food at about four weeks old.

The hippo stops drinking its mother's milk at about ten months old.

Female hippos start to breed at around four years old. Males must wait until they reach the age of ten. Rival males fight for the right to mate.

Hippos can live to around 35 years old. Most die of old age instead of being killed by predators.

Hippo Topic Web

GEOGRAPHY
- Mapwork: where hippos live
- Water: rivers and lakes
- Tourism: safaris
- Food journeys

ART
- Shape and movement
- Water in art

SCIENCE
- River, lake and grassland habitat
- Classification: mammals
- Adaptation to habitat: hippo's body shape
- Heat: evaporation and dehydration
- Animal groups: herd
- Hippo's life cycle
- Food chain and pollution

ENGLISH & LITERACY
- Meanings of names: scientific and common
- Write a story about a day in the life of a hippo
- Conservation debates

ICT
- Look at conservation groups' websites
- Send an email to the government expressing a point of view

MATHS
- Hippo numbers
- Height and weight comparisons

Extension Activities

English
- Debate whether hippos should be kept in zoos.
- Compare different information books about hippos.
- Think of different baby animal names, for example calf, cub, chick.
- Compare the names of different groups of animals, for example herd, flock, colony.

Maths
- Use the hippo's head as a model to develop work on symmetry.

Geography
- Trace a world map from an atlas. Show the location of Africa and the Sahara Desert.
- Draw a hippo distribution map.

Art
- Make a riverbank frieze, with basking hippos and other animals that share their habitat.

Science
- Make a chart showing how parts of the hippo's body are specially adapted for certain functions.
- Discuss the effect of global warming on the hippo and other river animals.

Glossary

Algae Simple plant organisms like seaweed.

Aquatic plants Plants that grow in or near water.

Antibiotic A substance that kills germs and prevents infection

Canine teeth Long, sharp pointed teeth at the front of the mouth.

Carnivore An animal that eats meat.

Dehydrate To lose water stored in the body.

Dominant The leading animal in a group, usually the most powerful and aggressive.

Endangered A species that is in danger of extinction.

Erosion Loss of soil and other material through constant wear.

Habitat The natural home for an animal or plant.

Herbivorous Animals that feed completely on plants.

Nocturnal To be active at night and sleep during the day.

Suckling Drinking milk from a mother's teats.

Territory An area of land that is controlled by an animal.

Further Information

Organizations to Contact

WWF-UK, Panda House,
Weyside Park, Godalming,
Surrey GU7 1XR
Tel. 01483 426444
Website: www.wwf-uk.org

Care for the Wild International
1 Ashfolds, Horsham Road,
Rusper, West Sussex TH12 4QX
Tel: 01293 871596
Website: www.
careforthewild.org.uk

Websites

Eyewitness PBS kids
www.pbs.org
A site with information about hippos and other wild animals.

The Discovery Channel
www.discovery.com
Use the search engine to find out information about hippos.

Books to Read

Heavy and Light by Rod Theodorou and Carole Telford (Heinemann, 1996)

The Hippo: River Horse by Christine Denis-Huot (Charlesbridge, 1994)

Nature Encyclopedia (Dorling Kindersley, 1998)

What is a Mammal by Robert Snedden (Belitha Press, 1997)

Index

All the numbers in **bold** refer to photographs or illustrations.